Lilies on the
Deathbed of Étaín
and Other Poems

Lilies on the Deathbed of Étain and Other Poems

OISÍN BREEN

Words copyright © 2022, 2023 Oisín Breen.
Typesetting and book design copyright © 2023 Downingfield Press Proprietary Limited.
All rights reserved.

Without limiting the rights under copyright reserved above, in accordance with the Copyright Act 1968 (Commonwealth of Australia) no part of this publication may be reproduced, stored in or introduced into a retrieval system, or transmitted, in any form or by any means (electronic, mechanical, xerographic, recording, or otherwise), without the prior written permission of the copyright owner and the publisher of this book.

Oisín Breen asserts their right to be known as the author of this work.

First published January 2023
Acquired and published September 2023 by
DOWNINGFIELD PRESS PROPRIETARY LIMITED
Suite 346
585 Little Collins Street
Melbourne Victoria 3000

mail@downingfield.com · www.downingfield.com

Downingfield Press undertakes its work on the unceded lands of the Wurundjeri people of the Kulin Nation and pays respect to Elders past, present, and emerging.

ISBN 978-0-6452318-1-6

Cover design by M. G. Mader

 A catalogue record for this work is available from the National Library of Australia

*To those who we have lost,
to those who are still with us,
to those we help stand,
and to those who help us to do so.*

Introduction

What of Lilies on the Deathbed of Étaín?
Well... it has been a whirlwind.

Its genesis lies in a particular moment, namely when I saw my oldest friend's grief crack through like a torrent as he laid his mother to rest. The inescapable love he showed, the stand-up quality he projected through the day, the laughter ... all that vanished for one perfect moment when sorrow washed over and through him, ecstatically. When I saw it happen, being a writer, I couldn't help but take note, and hold fast the word that followed in its wake, bouncing around my brain: godstruck. He was godstruck and it was beautiful. It drove the writing of the first poem of this collection, which details, from several perspectives – and multiple temporal instances – the wholeness of a life of a mother figure, through myth and realities, contemporary and past, as she is seen by others (and at times as she sees herself) in youth, age and in death. I'll confess, when I finished it, and then shared it with him, eager to see what he thought, there was a nervousness that was upon me, or at least working the edges of my mind, given the sensitivity of the subject – I had not asked his permission to write this piece – but his support for it was a real boon and wonder.

The book, this book, which contains one other long form work – Ana Rua, a sonic and formally experimental work addressing love, plain and simple – and some shorter works, too – detailing everything from Donegal migrant labour and potato farming in Scotland, to psychologically traumatised ducks, and an anti-love poem detailing an affair that did not happen – well, this book, like I say: whirlwind. It was picked up early 2022, and slated for publication, then published early 2023, although its actual launch caught me by surprise. It swiftly began hoovering up some pretty stellar reviews, too, for which I'm endlessly grateful, and a whole swathe of readers, many of whom I am delighted to have had the fortune of corresponding with. Yet, soon after its publication, the publisher closed suddenly, orphaning the work in its still early days, alongside that of many other excellent writers of the Irish and international avant-garde. Truly this was a damned shame, for a number of reasons, but in the great hunt to find someone to help breathe fresh life into this collection, one publisher stepped up with a great combination of understanding, affability, seriousness, professionalism and a willingness to bet on the quality of much of the current Irish/Irish-adjacent avant-garde, for which I am endlessly thankful.

Downingfield have been excellent partners in creating this second edition, which I am proud to share with you, the reader, who I must also, of course thank. The hat, well, it's firmly tipped.

Holding your second book in your hand, as an author is a different feeling to doing so with your first. The first time round, you're simply elated, there's a my god, oh god thank you! It is! It is! One's second work, well it has a certain alright, now we're talking, now we're going. With this republication the feeling is one of gratefulness, happiness, and a little bit of, alright, let's go, let's get harder, let's push more... and it's a wonderful feeling. So, again, my thanks.

On the work itself, some have spoken as to whether my doctoral work influences this book, and, well, the short answer, is not particularly, and probably, and it's the same all the way through all the influences and potential influences on this work. I hope it stands alone as what it is, but doubtless aspects of life, being, knowing, and all that jazz, well... they creep through, beautiful weeds wrapped round the base of the grapevine, and since everything requires relationality to function, I'll praise those weeds, too. But, put bluntly, the ambition for my work is that it is its own, that it is itself, that it carries magic, or wonder, that it plays, that it sings, that musicality pushes itself to the fore, that it is fire and passion, and most of all that it is absolutely not about the artist, but about the work and the subject. Famously, poets have been described as unacknowledged legislators, and more recently there has been a push for 'authenticity' and the representation of the personal 'real'. I respect the former and dismiss the latter. I believe poetry is based on artifice, and though it may borrow from the real, its falsehood allows it to speak to greater truth, and I hope, here, that I have succeeded in doing so, in some small measure at least.

Oisín Breen

Lilies on the Deathbed of Étaín

I

All this ends with the hocking of soft skin in loose folds,
A solemn current of spooled ink,
A stuffed portent:
That elegiac parchment of cause and effect,
And rhapsody, where each stroke of the hand
Is delicate enchantment.

Yet, like stripling vines in stupor,
We wrest ourselves from a standing start,
Only so as to glut ourselves, keening in the play of rustling air.

And, like children caught in first blush,
At rush to gorge our nascent wanting,
We relentlessly feast on the contingencies
That differentiate stone from stave.

But the salted oceans we pillage render up scant grain,
And illumination is in death, annihilation
And the hard sense of knowing:

      Curtain-fall and the committal.

How I long then for the pure milk of the word;
How I long then for the fine yew of the wood;
A caress, wet with a tongueful of discarded apocryphae.

Though, as I imagine her, the softness and the hardness;
The headiness and the fineness;
Her eyes: age, writ in the bark of an unhallowed kindness
Ground, too, in an Omertà of forgetting;

As I imagine her,
 she who was always the first;
 she who was poisonous, bearing bright red fruit;
Ioho, driving her crown unknowing into her wounds;

Ah Christ,
As I imagine it – cleaved from her –
This is the loss of plenty.
This too is a choral reliquary; a continuum in three parts:
Repetition, and a long harsh residue of sweetness and light;
Hard lye, asphalt dye in a mercantile air,
And an inching juggernaut of vapour.

This too is the laughing melancholia of the depths,
Where songbirds describe our stuttered movements,
With heavy breath and patternings of plucked strings –
  abeyance –
And the heat undoes me.

Yet here, murmurations and sow herds
Mingle at rest upon the rocks –
  jagged flagstones with fire beneath –
And with them, rent, is a holiness of measure –
  a panacea for the lengthiness of weight;
  for the edifying stillness of the grave.

And here too: Baile and Ailinn, in grief's pallor,
Leave each other scalped likenesses, eyeless messages,
Hooked in a tangle of bark-spattered joins.

> "And sure, the last picture I have of my uncle,
> he's dolled up like Napoleon Bonaparte," I says.

> "And sure, the hard ceramics of the endless
> stacks of the dead give me shivers," I says.

> "And sure, when I saw the man himself, sundered and wailing, when she, shorn
> of reminiscence, gobbled up the last of her air, wasn't I half heartbroken and half
> in love?" I asks.

> "But the only time I cried at a funeral
> was for someone I never really knew."

Yet the seasons mingle with the Boyne's black waters,
Where once the sun stood still for nine months
To placate the husband of the white cow, bou-vinda,
For Aengus, his birthright the Brug na Boinne,
Starfire on the longest day,
And for the thorn-struck blindness of Midir.

For each of us it differs.

Aengus' paid with the body of Étaín,
  his horror Fúamnach who spun Étaín
    to water, worm, and scarlet fly.
  his reprieve, her second birth in her thousandth year.
  his sentence, how Fúamnach lost her head.

For each of us it differs.

But our death will come in a single reckoning,
  a blow that shakes us from navel to heart,
  a furious meeting of synapses riffing out sketches
  in a stop-start-stop algorithmic play,

All at once,
And not at once.

And I have been dying for such a long time.

II

There is, however, a verse that is incumbent on us to repeat:
 of blessed hunger,
 and enduring until we die.

But I long for the pure milk of the word,
I long for the fine young yew of the wood,

> a caress, softly indulgent,
> and yet without measure,
> a kiss shared at Dromahair Bridge.

But it is beyond me,
And it is winter now,
And you, the young, must leave the old bereft.

Theirs is a rapture of russet,
Of left-behind apricot seeds,
A litany of gyres, levers and warning signs.

> THUS THE LEVEE SKIRLS WITH WHITE NOISE AND ELAN
> FOR HERE IN THE DARK LIGHT,
> WHERE PROHIBITION BECOMES LICENCE
> HERE THERE IS DEATH:
> THE ONE TRUE VISION OF ABUNDANCE.

Thus I keep traces of their names
 in the gabble of the yarrow stalk –
 in hexagrams –
 so as to lay down the power of them in memory.
 to cut the words of them in eight parts for the wooing of Étaín.
 to venerate them, and the shame of their cold-blood.
 to salute the traces of scarlet on their breasts.

And well I remember how she was
When I first saw her:

> bright silver she was.
> hair like a blooming iris.
> a beautiful painted corpse.

And after her second birth, she wed Eochu Airem.
But his brother wept for want of her, he wept
Until Midir tore him from his frame and took her three times.

So now *you* are my constant companion,
And I have made you a small chamber
So you might come and go.

And now I tell you:

This wet soil, from which I fashioned you a sleeping coat,
It is heavy with meal-worms.

This heat of yours, it will fire my body,
This instrument of lilies.

III

I tell you yet though:

It came in a single reckoning,
  a blow that shook me from the navel to the heart,
  a furious meeting of synapses riffing out sketches
  of a stop-start-stop algorithmic play

It was all at once,
  and not at once.

So I tell you:

I have been dying for such a long time,
  and I have seen its end.

It was like moss on the south face of the wall
  in the northern hemisphere;

Or thyme growing errantly on the windowsill opposite where you
  have your morning coffee, that hard gavel grinding earthiness
  tapping out notes of odour on a punch clock upon which time
  maps out not the limp unforgiving sermon of the wasted hours,
  but an aria of three-foot weather-worn signage that recounts all
  the places we have been and loved; where pigeons peck the
  grains on the grey cement, and old men sup soup through
  food-flecked beards telling each other – *'if they did, shite, I'd
  laugh me hole off'* – *'He was out there and ... it was ridiculous ...
  like 22 year-olds chatting me up'* – *'He's just, you'll have to ask
  him'* – *'ah but here she comes...'*

Or it was where scoliosis stitches up once beautiful women into
  the shape of feuding Christmas birds; and where I once sat
  hammering out inconsistencies, where others fled to the soft
  arms of pretty girls as a means to find a rum-soaked
  chin-splitting escape that happened to the clock, every fourteen
  years; and where I held hands and felt whole, totally and utterly
  whole.

It was like following a raggedy dog with the tremors,
  its parting breath overdue, but it unwilling to sunder itself from
  loving, even while lost in the thorny mountains of northern
  California; or the kind of idle happenstance that leaves you
  wildly obsessing over the beauty of someone, knowing they're all
  caught-up in the same mutual eulogy of brittle hunger and
  sharp, fast, hang-dog wasting-into-wanting for a taste or a bite
  on the slenderness of the nape of the neck or the shoulder –
  wildly too aware that now is not the right time, for you're
  already in love, though it's the right time for them – then for
  you, and not for them – so you go on wanting and wanting in
  asyncopatic rhythm, so you might as well just fill yourself
  hoarse on the fluttering breeze of the moments when you
  almost meet – O Étaín – or the day you – do you remember? –
  the day you were sitting at home drawing in a picture book till
  your father lifted you up and threw you out the front door
  telling you how the sun is a haven that spares you from regret,
  and this then led you to roaming till – as the sun climbed-down
  from its screeching perch – you went to gather flowers to give to
  your mother on time for tea, only to be met by her howling.

You were gone and she did not know why, she did not know where, and she was
  chewed up by the fear that you'd be gone before her.

It was like the faint memory of a jolting shuddering heave that
  left me in the back of a car, covered in broken glass and
  drowning in purple beet-stains, after a bus clattered into the
  back of us, and we on the way to the centre for the deaf – for I
  could not hear – but then seeing the faces of my mother and the
  driver convulsed into the rotten death-masks of neolithic
  soldiers burned by fire, for they saw death, a shattered husk –
  in infancy – torn from life by nothing other than the steady
  melody of idle chance; and it was like us laughing together, her
  having heaved me from herself, then stunned me, first with her
  wisdom, then with her ignorance.

Yet though it came in a single reckoning,
  a blow that shook me from the navel to the heart,
  a furious meeting of synapses riffing out sketches
  of a stop-start-stop algorithmic play,
It was all at once,
  and not at once.
And I have been dying for such a long time.

So this then is the mulch,
The one true elegy to the halter and the hare.

This is the silence of cacophony: the threnody to a saturated life,
Where Eochu Airem was forced to choose his wife from fifty,
Where – ignorant of her, after decades long spent wanting the
  sight of her – and she plump with child – this is where he
  chose, instead, his own daughter as his bride.

This, too, is where she bore his last son, then watched her
  husband-father burn, she the Mess Buachalla,
  as is writ in the yellow book of Lecal.

Here then, the beast is holy, the haar is holy,
  and holy too is the red honey,
  so too are lips, each others',
  especially *yours*,
  for which I have such a thirst.

IV

But now, the air outside us is sharp, and heavy with moisture,
  and we start to walk,
  and we match each other's rhythm,
  a pair of lust-drunk metronomes,
  where getting to know you better
  is the unthreading of a well-worn coat,
  and gripping your waist thrills,
      – ardour –
  never having realised the reach of one arm swallows you,
  or how small that makes you,
  and how hungry that makes me;
  and I am *so very* hungry.

It is October, late in the month.
It is always dark here.

Sometimes the darkness cleaves fulsomely, anxiously.
Others, it hangs on your eyelids like heat:
  exciting, soporific, but most of all an incantation to burrow
  into each other's skin.

It is late October, and we walk, in syncopated beat,
  until we stop; until we can not stop.

I turn to you, or you turn to me, or is it that we both turn
  to each other? And I don't want to say, and neither do you.

Think instead, of when a person looks at the stars.
On a clear night, far from the city, it is so different.
In the desert, sand noticeably cooling underfoot,
You retreating to the fire, it differs too.

There the sky is a hearthful of embers and surging starlight;
  pulsars slashing at the skin of the coarse grain; and a muddy
  filament lovingly wiped clean with a sweaty rag – the sky – the
  sky ruptures into a tendentious play for infinitude, where every
  star visible to the naked eye ushers in another in a finite but
  uncountable distribution of connection.

But your eyes do not unsheathe stars.

Instead, I see the sclera held tight in a pink and muddy pair of lids, softened by brushed browns and purples; irises refracting into ash, and pupils sharp as needlepoints, expanding and contracting, like the beating wings of an antler moth – a seductive scansion of the unuttered – driven by fibrous muscle and blood in a trabecular meshwork exhaling reservoirs of stillness and thirst.

But when I see this, I see also a fluid lattice, composed of fixed points in fixed rotation, entangled in the rupture engulfing your watchfulness with light and thought and wanting; and, as I turn to you, the patterns fuse – in lock-step – and the syncopated beat of doubled movement, stalled, instead becomes a diffusion of caterwauling rapture in the humming of shared sight.

It is October, and the cold humid air embalms your night-grey skin in a raised relief of plucked pores, tautened sinews and erubescent cheeks.

It is October, and I loosen the slack of my grip, almost shaking you free of me, leaving my palm resting on the top of your hip, and my fingers, feather-like, roiling the damp air just above your skin, a soft breeze through friction, and an insistence of momentary sensation that is almost, but not quite, touch.

Then you nearly buck, first at the sudden slackness, and then at the shivering I'm forcing into the small of your back – heavier now – twisting into a contrapposto pendulum of hip pressed with hip; hands now touching each other's waists; us turning into each other, from side to side circling through side, listing under the light and the air and the dawning weight of closeness, of smells, of colour and of taste.

Now think.

When you watch a candle – its balletic fire a torrent of seemingly
unending heat, a sharp fixed point of gulped air – silence meets
a breathless rhapsody of death, and there are instants of
stillness: moments where the flame flickers out, then continues;
they backed by equal moments of surging light, where blue
flickers – in milliseconds – venomously cohere, then vanish – a
traceless soliloquy of continuance.

Now think of when you fall into lock-step, together – a shared
pattern of touch and thirst – there too exists a tumult, a
withering and blooming of stopped hearts, and it coils around
you, until you become inseparable from its centre, and your
touch becomes theirs, and their touch another's, and the
distance between you is impossible to maintain, and there is
tension – your whole body a trap – primed – and you need to
and have to and ought to and should do and will do – you must
find release – and when you do, I flickers out, then continues –
and there is the light – *there is nothing else but the having and
the being had* – and everything vanishes in the desperate cerise
of pressed lips and curled lips, and rolling tongues; the
pressure of hands on your back, on the nape of your neck, on
the back of your head, running down the side – *gently* – of your
face – *and the light it is pulsing* – or your chest, or your breasts,
or your hips – *there is nothing else but having and being had* –
and you vanish into the parenthesis of pressure, of lolling
tongues and flaring nerve endings – interconnected – *and the
light it is blinding* – and there is always that continuance, that
message: *I want, I want, I want;* and further touch – *and the
light, I am reeling* – AND YOU ARE LOCKED NOW NOT IN
MOMENTS BUT IN NEED – *and the light it is everywhere* – and,
in the insatiable thrill of having, of you have and you do, and
you must have more, you do, and you drink, and you must.

It is October, and the sharp sting of the frozen wind electrifies,
and traces, in tandem with your tongue, the small creases of
age between my shoulder and my neck.

It is October, and we are drinking from each other, and it is impossible to stop.

V

Yet I am, I was, I will be, and I will not be.
The same is true for you.
We are born and we die.

And she is, she was, she will be, and she will not be.
This is as true for our mothers as it is for our fathers.
Everyone we love must die.

Know then that grief enacts its pallor on us relentlessly.

Death is a snare, we the trapped hare – senses in lieu of limbs bared like torn muscle in steel jaw-traps – suffering under a merciless gloaming of the soul that racks even the flesh of children at play – they in pirouettes – those shadow dancers in the dusk of harvest time – realising in one long day they'll race each other's heartbeats to a standstill, pull flecks of hay from each other's temples, laughing; then one of each pair will fatten with the weight of another marked utterance of life wrought unto being – for they, like us – hareish – watch the fires burn and traps snap shut – senses in lieu of limbs – racked with fulsome distemper, with each mile fled marked by a funereal stone.

But one marker is harder to traverse than the rest, because when your mother dies the tether snaps, and you know something is gone that will never return.

But in loss there is also the renaissance of stillness: one heartbeat in which to live, one vision, one mind, and a coalescence – our footsteps illumined by what we may yet become.

SO WITH ONE HEARTBEAT
ONE STEADY MOMENT OF EXULTANT PLEASURE
IN RAPTURE
I AM BECOME THE SUM OF MY PARTS
AND BEYOND THAT
THE END ANEW TO END

And I traipse, idly, with the same pitter-patter mind as the
 marsh tits that scavenge for scraps at the top of Leith walk,
 rambling down Broughton Street, and East Claremont Street,
 and St. Marks Path over the water, thinking of the great stone
 bridge and where you drink the waters to stave off the scythe;
 death-schlepping myself down Warriston road, accompanied by
 the sound of screeching gulls.

And here, by Crow Bridge,
 her red shoes and frame of purple
 stone guarding the twilight,
I like to walk.

It is peaceful, after all, here among the dead.
For those who come to mourn,
Shew their rent hearts at their openmost in sight.

And here, I once saw the face of God.

Here, Ailill Angubae, brother of Eochu Airem split himself into
 sherds to leave a portion of himself always watching over their
 mother, she who died of grief and memory lost after the
 burning of her second son.

Here, Ailill still stands vigil, too, and once,
When I went to the crematorium, I saw him,

        Godstruck

And his was the face of God,
And that lamenting voice, his too
That song of skin sung to the pilgrim's heady melody.

He was laughing,
Telling stories about her,
And he couldn't stop smiling.

Then the curtain fell.
The committal.

Then he fell.

He snapped;
  he, a twig under the hunter's boot;
  he, a reed torn by a careless child;
  he, later gathered by a mother duck to build a nest;
  he, bereft of she beyond forgetting;
  she who had, through illness, long since forgotten him,
  she whose love was without end,
  until it was pregnant with ending
  and imbued of ash.

> SO WITH ONE HEARTBEAT
> ONE STEADY MOMENT OF EXULTANT PLEASURE
> IN RAPTURE
> I AM BECOME THE SUM OF STARS
> AND BEYOND IT
> THE END ANEW TO END

He fell.
Motherless.
Motherless.

He fell.
And I have never seen anything so beautiful.

VI

It was beautiful the day she died.

She barely spoke.
But when she did, she asked after her childhood friends,
And I told her they were all long dead, and she the last.

All dead, buried beneath the Brug na Boinne: Aengus, he who
  was starfire on the longest day; the white cow, bou-vinda;
  thornstruck blind Midir; and mad Fúamnach of the water,
  worm, and scarlet fly; even Eochu Airem and his brother, Ailill
  Angubae, he who split into sherds, a portion of himself at vigil
  to wait for the passing of Étaín.

All dead, and there I stood,
At vigil in the resting place of the face of God,

And she sang then a childhood of whooper swans, and pochards,
Tufted ducks, and common terns;
Curlews, buzzards, ring necked ducks, and buff bellied pipits,
Sandpipers, great crested grebes, and blackcaps,
Heron, peeweeps, treecreepers, and the water rail.

She sang too of the pipit's soft electric whistle,
  and the inching horse whinny trill of the little grebe.

And I, half mad with grief,
I was convinced her final gasp was to be an epiphany.
But at her last she was displaced in time.
Each epiphany in two parts:

> *An inward breath, then an outward breath:*
> *the last raiments of white hot life.*

And she sang of the pipit's soft electric whistle,
And the inching hoarse whinnying trill of the little grebe.
Her last words thus a wet rhapsody of distorted breath,
One holy dream of ash scattered on the river Annalee.
And she told me her first kiss was in late autumn,
On a bed of wet grass and yellowing leaves by the hazel trees.

It was evening, and there was scarce traffic
Over the Dromahair Bridge,
Just the breath of young lovers,
And the rich fluting of the blackcap's crescendo.

And she told me:

Nine trees hang over the river,
Each dropping their fruit unto its black water.
And every afternoon, old Mary clambers along the banks,
Filling her pockets with hazelnuts,
Her good eye fixed on the O'Reilly,
He, the doyen who caught a salmon, where no salmon swim.

And she told me:

I fished for pike, perch, roach, the eel,
For trout, bream, trench, minnow, and rudd.
But that was not on the Dromahair, that too was on the Analee,
Where once I caught a lamprey eel: the thorn kisser,
And then spent the night with Mary,
Guzzling hazelnut and hawthornberry stew.

But Christ, my fear of being motherless could not stay my sleep,
And I dreamt, instead, of supping stew at the end of the world;
Of Bile Ratha, who guards the hazel tree;
Of new brides gifted catkins;
And of a forest flush with birth.

Then her chest burst with long twining branches, full in a livery
 of simple greens, embroidered with the wicked pulsing of red
 filbert fruit in a crimson crown, and flowering aments in yellow
 hue.

But by the Dromahair river, she said,
The air sharpening, and heavy with moisture,

  having walked in rhythm, he gripped my waist,
  and I never realised how the reach of his arm swallowed me,
  and how hungry that made me, and how hungry I was.

And the coming darkness cleaved fulsomely, anxiously,
It hung on my eyelids like heat, she said.
Her breath was susurrating leaves, and she chanted of the past:
An incantation to wallow in his skin:
An incantation of plucked pores, erubescent cheeks,
Of bucking, and shivering to the touch;
An incantation of hip pressed to hip,
Of the thirststruck, listing in the twilight;
An incantation of nothing else but having, and being had.

And she told me:

I have and I do, and I must have more and I do and I drink and I must, and still
       it is that I must drink and I do, I do, I do.

Then her chest burst with long twining branches full in a livery
of simple greens, embroidered with the wicked pulsing of red
filbert fruit in a crimson crown, and flowering aments in yellow
hue.

And to a drumbeat of breathless water, she fell still.
And nine trees hung over the river,
Each dropping their fruit unto its course,
And every afternoon she clambers along its banks,
Filling her pockets with hazelnuts,
And poaching salmon where none swim,
But that was not on the Dromahair, that was on the Analee,
Where she and I guzzled hazelnut and hawthornberry stew.

It was beautiful the day she died.

> BUT NOW THE LEVEE SKIRLS WITH WHITE NOISE AND ELAN.
> FOR HERE IN THE DARK LIGHT,
> WHERE PROHIBITION BECOMES LICENCE
> HERE THERE IS DEATH:
> THE ONE TRUE VISION OF ABUNDANCE.

SO WITH ONE HEARTBEAT
ONE STEADY MOMENT OF EXULTANT PLEASURE
IN RAPTURE
I AM BECOME THE SUM OF STARS
THE END ANEW TO END
AND SO IT IS
WE WILL BREAK THIS MESH THAT BINDS US
WE WILL BREAK THIS MESH THAT BINDS US
WE MUST AND WE WILL

The Love Song of Anna Rua

I

Ha-ra-hao-	Ha-ra-hao-	Rah-Hao-	Ha-Rah-Hao-
Ha-ra-rao-	Ha-ra-hao-	Rah-Hao-	

    All poetry is songliness,

        AND IT IS SHATTERING-

Tse-Tse-Tse-

        Like the ringing out of arias,

Ha-ra-hao-

        Hung out from the balcony.

Tse-Tse-

    Songs,
        They are like the ringing out of arias,

    Like red sheets:
        Falsettos
        From the window flung.

    Songs,

    They are built to crescendo,

    So as to;
    So as to;
    So as to lick themselves clean,
    Their skirts lifted,
    While their necks crane,
    So as to tongue the instep of their soliloquous feet.

> Feet, which we know only as shadows of images,
> Left behind disturbances,
> In the guise of waves
> Of a sound.

Mai-   Mai-ha-ra-ma   Mai-ha-ra-ma-way-wahama
Mai-ha-ra-ma-way-wahama-whup-tama

Mai-ha-ra-ma-way-wahama-whup-tama-way

> Sound.
> Gorge on our shedding skin.
>
> All this has happened,
> And all this that has happened is new.
> It is new, and I and you again
> Have differing personalities become:
>
> Synecdoches of an other,
> Heavenly choral somnambulists,
> Filling the air with singular melancholias,
> Like the ringing out of arias-
>
> AND THIS IS HOW WE BEGIN AGAIN.
> WE BEGIN AGAIN WITH EUPHORIAS,
> GLORIAS, MORATORIA, AND OUR FOOTSTEPS,
> WHICH JUST NOW HIT A BEAT.

Mai-   Mai-ha-ra-ma
Mai-ha-ra-ma-way-wahama-whup-tama-way

> Like the ringing out of arias,
>
> THIS IS HOW WE BEGIN AGAIN.

Mai-ha-ra-ma-ha

> We share the same set of keys,
> To the same set of doors.

The same set of dreams:
>Baleful ones,
>Those soulful ones, those long meaningful ones –
>Dreams which gather yet in parliaments.
>Dreams that gather under the benevolent eye
>Of the slumbering God,
>A God whose pet crows hiss like snakes.

We share the same grave,
Yet, that which we do not share,
It is flowering.
We do not share an epitaph.

And what we do not share is flowering.
We do not share an epitaph,
And mine is dressed only so as to assert:

Independence, mine,
And the certainty of that laughter
I last saw in the mountains,
>when I pretended to be a deer and slipped;
>when you shouted at me,
>while all I thought of
>was the whetting of my thirsty beak.

Anna- Aye-	Aye-Anna-	Aye-Anna-

It is a sad thing to think on,
Before we begin again.
It is sad to think that we imagined.

Aye-	Aye-	Aye-Anna-

Yet here I am,

>And HERE you *are*.
>Spectral, grinning, making daisy chains from the past tense, and in verse throwing shapely flowers: a sepia existence that may never be expunged.

Yet here we are,

AND THE GODS THEY ARE BENEVOLENT.

>   Bloody, ashen maybe, in sack-cloths, yes, but
>   with calloused fingers, finding yet again another
>   way to bridle time for another ring-around-the-

Roh-   Roh-   Roh-Aye-Anna-

Yet here I am in the city.
Where, like aeroplanes,

> SOUND

The street-sweepers of the morning,
Theirs the boiler's din.

And rigor mortis

> SETS

In my fantasies at least,
And I turn to thoughts of birth and being born,
And I solidify.

> One creature –
> Divine and elementary –

Yet here I am,
Plucking at the silhouette of moments,
Watching the roots again stir.

And the names of things,
Previously not particular to me,
Retooled in a new garb of haunting,
Settle beneath my bones.

And the weak forces that hold my universe together

Quicken,
        Quivering
                Cognisant

To a re-ordering power:
        The hushed lilt of love-love-love

And it is rampant:

        A new theodicy
        Rewritten only so as to supersede its former self.

And here I am,

Mai-ha-rama   Mai-ha-rama   Mai-ha-ra-ma-way-

    To sing in the new.

        Crushingly,

        With benevolent opposition,

To shatter the palms of past kindliness.

II

But you know that we do not share an epitaph.
And you know that all this has happened,
That birth is the long-tail of death;
That all that has happened is new,
And is new since I and you
Have again differing personalities become.

And your tenderness,
So sculpted,
Has become that refined shape:
The phantasmagoria.

        It is distended,
        Wrought.

And, like so much that is old,
From its patchwork of tattered skin,
Not all of it is yours.

And your simplicity,
So tempered –
Reified –
Has become a tabernacle of entropy.

        It is gushing
        Holiness

    And, at its extent,
    It is the suffering of fools,
    With all of us on all fours,
    And you are NOT a benevolent god.

Ha-ra-hao   Ha-ra-hao   Ha-rah-hao

  Like the ringing out of arias,

Tse-Tse-Tse

    So, in the hollowed out gills,
    Of the aquamarine necks
    Of those who have forever waited,
    With breath baited,
    Your simplicity,
    Your tenderness,
    Snaps.

Anna-   Anna-   Anna-Rua

III

We share the same set of dreams:
Those baleful ones, those soulful ones,
Those long meaningful ones.
Those dreams which gather yet in parliaments.
Dreams which gather under the benevolent eye
Of the slumbering gods.
Gods whose pet crows hiss like snakes,
Only so as to warn Cú Chulainn of the waves,
Echoing into history
Their just and synaesthetic mirthfulness.

Yet,
For all this,
There exist those blacker thoughts:

Melancholias, forced fixed euphorias, thrills, spills, and hackneyed blue-eyed boys and girls who, sunning themselves, with ice-cream dripping down their noses, as their faux-saintliness has gravity itself inverted, conceive of nothing other than being like and unto one and other.

And though crafted from the coin one sided, illusion, though it pleases us, does not stand over reason, nor the turning of her hexagon onto the fattened heads of queens.

And thus,

Roh-   Roh-   Roh-Aye-Anna-Tse-

Thus, alike unto one and other,

We titter to each other, of the darkness.
We titter to each other, doleful, baleful, soulful dry-

How:
        'It is *always* beautiful.'

How:
        'It is *always* beautiful and the same.'

How:
        'It is always beautiful *because* it is the same.'

And though clipped, cobbled from that coin so sided,
reason, though it pleases us, can not supplant
submission, nor the turning of the hexagon onto the
panoptic sights of power.

        Like the Robin,
        An Spideog chróga,
        With breast blood red,
        Na Gaoithe rua leis an farraige,
        Ríthe an tsaoil uafásaich,
        With the only spectral permanence being change,
        Ins an áit ard na capaill, na crainn,
        Faoi thine na haigne
        Those born, still-born,
        Nuair a labhair na daoine Gaeilge
        Agus Béarla de lá agus d'oiche.
        This we can not know.
        Níl fhios agam.
        We can not know.

And from all this then,
There exist blacker thoughts:

Dubh-   Dubh-   Dubh-

Eruptions –
Cracked and pierced,
Eruptions –
Sounding out their openness
Like tins of cheap beer burst.

Dubh-Dubh-Dubh

Mai-ha-ra-ma   Mai-ha-ra-ma-way-wahama-whup-tama-

Mai-ha-ra-ma-way-wahama-whup-tama-way-

Mai-

    So it is for this,
    Just for this,
    That we exist.

        AND YOU HAVE PUT TENOR, TIMBRE,
        AND TIME TO OUR REMEMBRANCE.
        YOU ARE THE PRELUDE OF FORGETFULNESS.
        AND THIS IS THE MEASURE OF MIRTH.

    So here we are,
    Where we used to forage together for huckleberries,
    For blackberries and raspberries,
    For strawberries and seabuckthorn.

        IT IS HERE THEN-
        THAT THE MANY HEADED UNITY THRIVES

            That rough beast of Restoration,
            In perpetuity goring its coloured tail.

IT IS HERE THEN-

> HERE THAT YOU LUSTILY CHASE HER,
> YOUR CUP OVERFULL,
>
>> Her collapsed breasts
>> Echoing your sin.
>
> IT IS HERE THEN-
> HERE YOU MADE IO FEAST FOR FLIES
>
>> And here you too must kneel.
>>
>> Kneel.
>>
>> KNEEL

Mai-	Mai-ha-ra-ma-way-wahama-whup-tama
Mai-	Mai-ha-ra-ma-way-wahama-whup-tama-way

IV

Tse- Tse- Tse

        Na cailliní, dubh, Na buachuallí, dubh,
        An grá; dubh, mar níl faic na fríde againn.

Ha-rah-hao   Ha-rah-hao

    And all poetry is songliness-

    And now,
    With the curtains of mine billowing around the self of me,
    For winter it is,
    And the haar is strewn, suspended,
    Snowflakes of blurred vision in the air,
    With I, internally at least, an Iam elsewhere being,
    There is only one melody and one fervour that remains.

    And the only God is Love.

    AND THE ONLY GOD IS LOVE.

| Rua- | Rua- | Tá an saol (seo) againn rua. |
| Rua- | Anna- | Aya-anna-tse |

    And now,
    Much as the streets are heavy with noise,
    And your heart is heavy with beating,
    So too is history with meaning,
    And so too are the damp footsteps of the past
     with acts of disappearing,
    For in this singularity there exists more
     than only the many and the multitude.

    AND HERE, A THRONGING SLUMBER
    BREATHES SERRATED MINDFULNESSES,
    ALL DRESSAGE TO THE HOMILY
    OF MUSIC IN THE MAKING.

V

Do you remember then?

> How it's just like piano music?
> The way it cuts through your eyes?
> And how it left your irises
> Freshly spliced with tears?

This music,

> It is the rinsing of order out of void.
> The birthing of wonder,
> But it does not belong to us.
> And we glean the songlines from the stars
> From which, inviolably, beauty is born:

> A tremolo-

And yet,
If all song is poetry,

> AND IT IS MANY THINGS
> AND MANY HEADED

If it is not concrete, but is yet concrete,
If it is opaque and transparent both,
If it is religion and it is truth,
 both in sympathy and discord,
If it is not-
If it is,

Then I am wet at the thought of my thirst, and I drink
 down lusts and thoughts with the same fervour and
 animality as the lion mulling mauls its prey, and
 mothers guard their cubs.

If it is,

>Then my loving, artistry, and craft,
>All meanings which are of myself constituent,
>None are more than this:
>>a fantasy, which, with canny zeal, has stoked the fires inside me.

D'ith mé.	D'ith mé ceol an tsaoil.
D'ol mé.	D' ól mé na réaltaí.
Thóg mé.	Thóg mé póg amháin uait.

If it is,

Then that task which is for me, and only me is to – with endless hunger – rip the meat from symbols; knowingly spit difference; split hairs; and, between the I in me and the I in you, my task is to denote freedom, connote separation, and bellow out the song inside us.

Thus,
Since I hold that these conditions here are true.
We are caked in mud, and hot with ivy charred,
And it is out of melody, of song and making,
That we have all this upon these shared selves foisted.

Thus is it that the knowledge of our cooking, broiling, laughing sin and sinlessness was pumped down our hale and hearty necks.

Thus it is, at the behest of this melodic and temporal instantiation, that the coloured deities, powder-ground by the coarse mastications of the horse, were fed in pellets to the gulls, only so that we might have heaven always beneath our feet.

>I tread then not only on dreams,
>But on heaven herself.
>And thus it is then,
>
>NOW

That we must gulp down the feasting flies,
So that we might thrive,
With many eyes,
Plastic, priapic, yet alive.
And thus it is that the best of us,
At most an essential pulsing of light,
Can etch only moments on the walls of La Tène,
Wildly aware that all this has happened,
  and all that has happened is new.
It is new since I and you have again differing
  personalities become.

And we, with icy sinews,
We are a plague of the living,
Of verseless nationality,
Of a long short, long long short, dash
  in a garden of syntax-

Yet, though our beauty, like the hourglass,
  has long since been crushed, it remains,
  and it IS animating,
And it IS the agent of disruption.
It is in the stirrings of the cracking of eggs.
It is in the membrane,   harvested,
                                changed,
                                toughened,
Whose skin will not break.
And it is refuted solely in the ordinary,
And it is therefore not for you.

So here it is then.
The here and now.

Ha-rah-hao	Ha-rah-hao	Aye-Anna	Aye-Anna
Roh-	Roh-Anna-	Roh-Aye-Anna-Tse	

And we crack eggs,
Like our ancestors cracked skulls,
And we force ourselves to penetrate the light.

And though the bell tolls,
And my feet grow fungus and I am drunk,
And I still suffer,
Conflict is in meaning;
The relation between object and symbol;
Between the divergence of the I in the owner
 and the owned –

And, though we must eat the worms
Out of the bellies of our grandchildren;
Though I still kneel prostrate
Behind a nested set of identities,
I am without regret.
But here, behind the sands, transparent and mixed,
They of cowhide spun,
I, however, am unable to forget.
And in this lament,
Through which I am far from the living,
I am the coldness of the passing of the waves

> AND I AM UNABLE TO FORGET.
> BUT THERE IS MOVEMENT.
> THERE IS LIGHT
> WE ARE, AND WE IMAGINE,
> AND WE ARE VISIONARY THINGS,
> AND I AM, AND I EXIST,
> AND IT IS POSSIBLE
> TO LOSE ONESELF IN ELATION.

VI

I remember, too, that like so much that is old,
From a patchwork of tattered skin,
Not all of this is mine.

And I have fattened my gums on the carcass of memory.
My eyes have also burst
 at the sight of the gluttony ripened worm,
And I too have been like that masturbatory calf:

> golden in submission,
> while I waited for the eclipse,
> knowing that in sulphur I would bloom.

Yet I was unable to forget-
And I did not forget-

And then:
        An eruption
                An erupting
                          pounding
                                    beat –

The piano key

Anna-	Aye-Anna-	
Roh-	Roh-Anna-	Roh-Aye-Anna-Tse-

And in this transparency
My frayed feet do stamp up storms,
And the creatures of the laughing din
 bring flames.

Aye-	Aye-Anna-	Aye-Anna-
Roh-	Roh-	Roh-Aye-Anna-Tse

> And here the books are opened and they have
> spun thoughts and thoughtlessness, heeds,
> creeds, sanities, madnesses, and myopias,
> voyeurs, and newly formed distended prehensile
> thumbs on the racked bodies of inconsistency,
> and the thundering beat of that ruined inferno:
> melody.

| Aye- | Aye-Anna- | Aye-Anna- |
| Roh- | Roh- | Roh-Aye-Anna-Tse |

> Here is the fattened lamb of delirium.
> Feast. Feast. Feast.

| Aye- | Aye-Anna- | Aye-Anna- |
| Roh- | Roh- | Roh-Aye-Anna-Tse |

> And words are the epitome
> Of the physical and the real,
> And Lust is real.
> Hunger is real.
> Love is real.
> Your thirst is real.
>
> Feast. Feast. Feast.

| Aye- | Aye-Anna- | Aye-Anna- |
| Roh- | Roh- | Roh-Aye-Anna-Tse |

> Then-
> Into silence-
> And stillness-

> Where this stillness is derived from the succour of
> knowing, of knowing that the fast beat is
> followed by the slow.

| Aye- | Aye-Anna- | Aye-Anna- |
| Roh- | Roh- | Roh-Aye-Anna-Tse |

Then-
 Feet first,
 The fray entered,

This is the moment in which to announce,
With feet first:
IT IS
THIS IS
AND-

Aye-   Aye-Anna-   Aye-Anna-
Roh-   Roh-   Roh-Aye-Anna-Tse

Now-
Baulk.
Thrum.

> Sharp is the reply.
> Sharper still the message:
>
> That even horror can be healed-
> That indecision is exegesis-
> That what is malleable
> unites us in synthesis-
> While obsolescent sorrows are replaced by
> the falling parentheses –
> Not in light, but in laughter-

Now-

On the long leaves and loose gravel,

> In auburn,
> Those sharp tongues are dressed,

And your feet mind the memory of the heavenly ground,
And weightlessness, disturbed, is subsumed in surety.

Now-

Since we have, needs must,
Forged this delicate cosmetics,
To provide a new impetus for our beautiful dilemma,
With ice harrowed sinews,

	I strangle – I strangle her.		
Anna-	Anna-Rua-	Aye-Anna-	Roh-Aye-Anna-Tse-

THEN –
        I CHOKE
        IT, AND
        YOU, AND
        YOU SEE, AND
        YOU BECOME
        AGAIN AWARE:
        YOU ARE
        AN ERUPTION
        OF LIFE

Aye-	Aye-Anna-	Aye-Anna-
Rua-	Rua-	Roh-Aye-Anna-Tse-

Then the storm becomes stillness,
And the haar but one long syntax of last words
And I am breathless.

Aye-	Aye-Anna-	Aye-Anna-
Roh-	Roh-	Roh-Aye-Anna-Tse-

VII

Now,
Waterlogged and in colour,
Your irises are wet with insufficient space.
And, with the obelisk of cruelty glossed,
The hollow end of decision ghosts in the vertical
And the horizontal,
And the Geist, at harvest peak,
Finally answers back:

> 'YOUR HEAVY LIMBS HAUNT OUR SKINS
> AND, AS WE IMAGINE EACH OTHER ONLY
> FROM OUT OF THE OPAQUE, THE FAILURE
> OF LOVE IS THE FAILURE OF IMAGINATION.'

So it is that I cut decks.
I purvey symbols.

And we need only imagine then
That it is possible.

And I deal the hand,
And we start again.

Anna-	Aye-Anna	Aye-Anna-
Rua-	Rua-	Roh-Aye-Anna-Tse

VIII

The shot is exterior
A different room.
I enter.

She sits there.
Her eyes are tawny.
She is milk.

I am in a different room.
Being elsewhere I-
I am somewhere I have never been before.

She sits there.
Her eyes are tawny,
And everything has changed.

Her hair,
I examine it in the same way one might a horse's teeth,
And I ask myself,
Before considering this affair:

>'Is her head too small?'
>'And is she really married?'
>'Didn't I already meet him?'
>'Christ, he was really fucking ugly wasn't he?'

But none of this really happened,
If it did, I imagine
It doesn't matter.

I met her,
And all I could think of saying was:

I want to taste you,
And I want you to taste me.
I want to laugh with you,
And I want you to laugh with me.

Anna-	Aye-Anna-	Aye-Anna-
Roh-	Roh-Anna-	Roh-

And all poetry is song–

AND IT IS SHATTERING

Roh-Anna-   Roh-Anna-

Like the ringing out of arias,

Roh-   Roh-Anna-   Roh-Aye-Anna-Tse-

I want the cobblestones to be wet with rain,
Just to offer you my umbrella.
I want it to be cold,
Just so as to offer you my coat.

Roh-   Anna-Rua-   Roh-Anna-Tse-
Anna-

I want this year to become the next,
And the next, the one after that.

Roh-   Roh-Anna-   Roh-Aye-Anna-Tse-

I know that we are all on the threshold
Of imagination.
So we can begin again,
And although we do not share an epitaph,
Where there is an ending,
So too is there a start.

Roh-Anna-   Anna-Rua-   Anna-

And the weak forces that hold my universe together

    Quicken,
       Quivering,
          Cognisant

To a re-ordering power:
  That hushed lilt of love-love-love.

Anna-

    I turn again to birth.
    And it is rampant.

Anna-

    Under this staggering sky my laughter lilts.
    Under this living memory of melody:

      The fawn's chorus

    And again we cut each other's wings.
    Again we stain ourselves with wine,
    And again I catch its redness on my tongue,
    As it chases timelessness
    On the inside of your thighs.
    And there is light.

      Light. Light. Light.
      Built to a crescendo-

Rua- Rua- Rua-

  So as to –
  So as to –
  So as to imagine an end.

Six Months Bought with Dirt: the Bothy Crop of Arranmore

They knelt in the dirt, joining a movement gigaannum long,
A continuum shifted in increments by ancestral kin, and time
Transformed their role to architect, where once, like so many
Others of their wide-eyed and lust-hungry frame, they served
As co-conspirator among the heavy legged, who pound dirt
And stone as they run for warmth and nourished bone.

They knelt in the dirt, above the worms, and seedlings
Dampened off, pressing their hands beneath the earth, seeking
A grip – with fingertip traces – a hold on life, to pull
The tubers from the soil in April and in June, In late August
And October, too. And their fingernails were purple brown,
Those islanders, who knew the chopped yawl sail
From Burtonport to Arranmore and back.
Some dug, others gathered: a bothy crop.

They knelt in the dirt, whole families, who moved each year,
For like the swallow, whimbrel, and sandwich tern, they lived
To a steady pattern that spread its seed back-and-forth,
A kindling for change rippling out in knots of life
Clustered among the north-west islands
And the lowland fiefs of Dál Riata.
Their children kept the beat on water and lowland, too,
Singing of Baidín Fheilim, the boat broke off Tory.

They knelt in the dirt, and moved from farm to farm,
Gathering the crop – Yetholm Gypsies, Kepplestone Kidneys,
And Highland Burgandies – always singing of the little boat
The little boat that went away to Gola and then to Tory.
They knelt in the dirt, gathering their crop in baskets
Wicker woven – a chain-link from mud to young man's belly.
They slept in stone huts, too, hoarding silver in purses,
Their father's before, to take to kin in Arranmore.

They knelt in the dirt through summer and autumn,
Tattie hokers most, though some worked to furnish the others
With spun cloth, sharp knives, and with the few ministries
Of love that wind-whetted hearts could spare,
Before the morning's walk, miles of land stalked in service,
Dually done for barely known scions of the long-dug soil with marble
blemishes on alabaster skin, and for old mothers who sang to keep the heat in.

They knelt in the dirt, often singing, too, of Fheilimí beag,
Of his little boat with the fish aboard, and Fheilimí in it,
And the sea aboard beside Fheilimí.

They knelt in the dirt, stopping only to chew on soda bread,
Its crusts wet with last night's treat of dillisk soup,
A welcome weed, and water wine, dried in bags,
Kept beside their sleeping mats, having gathered it by moonlight,
Having gathered it as children, too,
On the storm-swept rocks of home.

And they sailed, at last, after months away,
To return to that resting place of tenderness.
And the sight of the yawl, holding steady
Above the waves, each washing the stone-guarded coast,
It was enough to still – for a season, at least –
That seed of melancholy for the surely lost and dead,
Brothers, sisters, all. And in its place came laughter,
And a ritual of held hips, and clasped hands, of sweat and drink,
All bought with fistfuls of dirt.

Six months toil for a kiss,
For a child's hand held,
Six months bought with dirt.

At Swim, Two Pair

In two directions then, they swim, mother, sister, and kin,
Their bodies half submerged in the gloaming, vespers sung,
And the water around them weaves eddies,
A nest of spent influences and serried trails,
Shivering outwards in concentric circles,
A plush map of hydrogen and oxygen blended,
And a platform for ambitions that span millennia,
For designs we also dearly hold, as passing seconds,
Marked by respiration, are measured in calls,
Calls that begin near the heart, as syrinxes swell.

Those calls are an act of flutistry, too,
Before the breaking branch of breath, as folds of flesh vibrate,
And waves of sound overlap – parallel to the current shift –
Through a tiny box of cartilage, scaled in millimetres:
A bone memory, and a fuselage formed of librettos shared,
With each an issuance of courting,
Rolled out in sets of two and ten,
Each pair softer than the last,
Each met equally by a distribution of rasping two note calls
And shrill whistles, which warn, and shepherd, too.
Yet, unfashioned for song, these calls, instead,
Prove spirit shaping sounds: a known quantity
Of convocated speech: the quale of river birds.

And they swim together, mother, sister, and kin, four abreast,
For weeks longer than they ought,
Two generations keening in motion,
Two pair, where once moved a score and six.

Yet for twenty days, the youngest two dozen of the brood,
It larger then, sheltered their water-wet crowns
Under a pair of common roofs, hewed out of protein
And hollowed bone. They sheltered under outstretched fibres
Of pleated skin, megaannum old, and, in form,
A living shadow guise: an echo of frilled throats slung back
To scream a lustrous piercing note: a step function
For the beating heart, and a last reminder of how silence shares
The significance of loss, even with those glutted flesh-fat bellies
Of the always death-near hunting birds,
And the long wearing down of polyphyodont teeth.

Yet for twenty days, the work of time became a meshwork of rest,
Of webbing spread, and hind legs, in haste, pushed back
And down, steadily pressing against the water in a silent rapture
Of movement, as two broods, grouped, lingered
Along Lough Foyle. And, when the first day was done,
It became, too, a tableau of soft sound,
As the youngest swiftly learned to forage, run, and swim,
A lesson, long a prelude for the water thirst, of 24,
As each saw, in the charred blemishes five years had left –
Time's trace – on their mother's face, a compulsion,
Likely a decade long, to push bodies below the water line,
To meet an ocean deep need to drink gallons,
Each alone, by the day.

They swim together now, mother, sister, and kin, four abreast,
For weeks longer than they ought, two pair, keening in motion,
Yet their damp rustling is but a bleary epilogue
Of talons hooking flesh, of hawk, owl, and gull,
Of otter, mink, and stoat, each eager to strike,
Each eager to sate a hunger known,
Even below by the dappled pike –
That burrowed maw of water song –
And its whirlpool gulps were the last brood blow,
Survived only by the four-strong testament it left behind:
Two pair in motion, where once moved a score and six.

A Chiaroscuro of Hunger

It was ten years ago, when she asked me
To serenade her. She sat beside Triton's fountain,
In Rome, as the sun-shook air near split with heat,
And small globes of water acrobatically landed
On my cheeks, red with the thought of a kiss.

And I could see the electricity, pulse, somehow,
In the whites of her eyes, and I knew everything
She wanted, and why she couldn't want it,
Even though she did, and she knew, looking at me,
That all she had to do was ask.

I was tired then, worn out by hundreds of poor choices,
And passions that burnt red hot, only to turn white hot,
And sunder skin from bone, prompting the perennial
Reassembling of fragments of a jigsaw puzzle,
That, at times, resembles my face.

Yet I sang to her, a song I learned in the woods that summer,
It was a love song about a tubercolic country girl,
In the twelfth century, whose father begged her to marry,
Who told him she would wait until he was dead,
Because he refused the man she loved.

And although my voice is patchy, at best, I can carry a tune,
The way old men do, in bars, where feeling matters more
Than technique. But when I thought of pressing my tongue
Against hers, I was careful in my fantasy to be delicate
And rough, the two extremes balanced by her breath.

We did not kiss, because she was faithful then, to a man
Who promised to take care of her, even when she wept,
As she often did, her ability to cope worn down
By the ministry of a father, who provided everything,
But could not love, nor teach her how to laugh.

We left then, to walk among the gardens of Barberini Palace,
And catalogue, together, an alternate history of marble
Statues, which came alive at night and revelled, wine-drunk
Recreating the memories we all must share in want,
And the tips of my fingers roiled for need of hers.

But we never touched, so careful were we to avoid it,
Even when we lay down together, on a long leather divan,
In the great hall, its paintings an excuse to study the artistry
Of blemishes, you learn through closeness, that fosters thirst
Beneath The bones. And together, we became a chiaroscuro
One of hunger in the heat:

An instance of fission
Suspended on the threshold of shared time.

Even Small Birds Can Render Planets unto Ash

The water chopped beneath us,
And the backwash of our salmon leap,
In the heavy sun,
Was a trail of crystals,
Refractions of brightness
Birthed into being
By shuddering jolts,
Each the ministry
Of diesel power.

And as the steel frame, which guarded us
From breathlessness, threw itself
Through thick arteries of hydrogen,
And oxygen, and coral-infused light,
On the starboard side, a circus of puffins
Bobbed on the breathing waves.

Some threw a fit of flight, and lifted, light,
Their slack frames into a furious fling-
-ing of black pistons moving through the air,
As if it were a heavy soup,
And their beating wings a great machinery
That could render even planets unto ash.

Yet it was the others,
In great improbabilities of scurrying new movement,
That left me gasping at their impetuousness
And vivifying life, as they paused, then ducked
Beneath the waves, only to rise unto an apex of white foam.

And their black wings beat against the lolling current,
Along the white lines that bifurcated the luminescent tunnels
Collapsing in their wake.

Acknowledgements

Firstly, my thanks to Mitchell and the whole team at Downingfield for their hard work, and their kindness, and understanding in working with both me, and a number of other Irish and international avant-garde writers orphaned after the sudden and rather messy collapse of an Irish publisher.

My thanks, also, to both Róisín Ní Neachtain, editor of Orphic Press, and Alan Gillis, poet and professor of modern poetry at Edinburgh University, who were early supporters of this work, and who were kind enough to provide a synopsis of their thoughts in 'blurb' form, for its first edition. You're both wonderful, and I certainly owe you both a pint.

I offer vast and further thanks then, to all those who have reviewed this work, too, including (and forgive me if I've omitted you, it's hard to keep a full track here) Robert Vollmar and Greg Brown of World Literature Today; Ryan D. Brinkhurst at Literary Heist; Paul Thompson; Joyce McMillan and Roger Cox at the Scotsman; Rajesh Subramanian; Rebecca Rijsdijk of Sunday Mornings at the River; Serena at Savvy Verse and Wit; Stephanie Gemmell at Inklette; J.S. Watts, for the High Window; Melissa Ridley Elmes for Tinderbox; JP Seabright and Leia Butler for Full House; Daunish Negargar at New Critique; Angela Maria Spring at the Washington Review of Books; Tiffany M Storrs and Kellie Scott-Reed of Roi Fainéant; Emma Lee; Denise Hill of New Pages; not to mention the sheer number of journals willing to get into the muck with interviews, podcasts, analyses, and those who are still reviewing and helping promote this work; and lord, thanks to each and every person that shouts this work out!

Secondly, I must also provide my thanks to the small independent journals and magazines that provided a home for a few of the poems, or an extract or two, carried in this book, they being, as follows:

Six Months Bought with Dirt: the Bothy Crop of Arranmore, first published in the An Áitiúil Anthology from the Martello and the Madrigal.

At Swim, Two Pair, first published by Lucent Dreaming.

A Chiaroscuro of Hunger, first published by the University of Birkbeck's Mechanics Institute Review.

I also owe my thanks to About Place, La Piccioletta Barca, Grub Street, Crow of Minerva (now Orphic), Meniscus, the Riverbed Review, and Stepaway Magazine.

During my writing process I often extract small snippets from my longer form works, play with them, rework them, sometimes even bash them together to form other wholes in a collage, and each journal and magazine was kind enough to publish one such work.

My thanks, too to Déirdre Ní Mhathúna, for helping make sure my Gaelic phrasing is up to snuff!

Lastly, I should also thank you, the reader for your kindness, and I hope that the musicality that I intended to bring forth with this collection has found an appreciative ear.

My Thanks.

Irish poet, doctoral candidate, and journalist, **OISÍN BREEN**, a multiple Best of the Net nominee and Erbacce Prize finalist, is published in 112 journals in 21 countries, including in *Agenda, North Dakota Quarterly, Books Ireland, About Place, Door is a Jar, Northern Gravy, Quadrant, Decomp,* and *The Tahoma Literary Review*. *Lilies on the Deathbed of Étaín* is Breen's widely reviewed and highly praised second collection. It follows his critically well received debut, *Flowers, All Sorts, in Blossom...* (Dreich, 2020).

www.ingramcontent.com/pod-product-compliance
Lightning Source LLC
Chambersburg PA
CBHW032018290426
44109CB00013B/700